IN THE NEWS Need to Know

Artificial Intelligence

by Ashley Kuehl

Consultant: Caitlin Krieck, Social Studies Teacher and Instructional Coach, The Lab School of Washington

Minneapolis, Minnesota

Credits

Cover and title page, © BlackJack3D/iStock; 4, © CPA Media Pte Ltd/Alamy Stock Photo; 5, © Seventyfour/Adobe Stock; 7, © Anadolu/Getty Images; 9, © Erik Isakson/Getty Images; 11, © tostphoto/Adobe Stock; 13, © CentralITAlliance/iStock; 15, © isa_Ozdere/Adobe Stock; 17, © adamkaz/Adobe Stock; 19, © DMP/iStock; 21, © Mix/Adobe Stock; 23, © Roman/Adobe Stock; 25, © The Washington Post/Getty Images; 27, © NurPhoto/Getty Images; 28TL, © Roberto Ricciuti/Getty Images; 28ML, © Anna Moneymaker/Getty Images; 28BL, © Jules White /Vanderbilt University

Bearport Publishing Company Product Development Team

Publisher: Jen Jenson; Director of Product Development: Spencer Brinker; Managing Editor: Allison Juda; Editor: Cole Nelson; Associate Editor: Naomi Reich; Associate Editor: Tiana Tran; Art Director: Colin O'Dea; Designer: Kim Jones; Designer: Kayla Eggert; Product Development Specialist: Owen Hamlin

Statement on Usage of Generative Artificial Intelligence

Bearport Publishing remains committed to publishing high-quality nonfiction books. Therefore, we restrict the use of generative AI to ensure accuracy of all text and visual components pertaining to a book's subject. See BearportPublishing.com for details.

Quote Sources

Page 28: Nigel Shadbolt from "AI Safety: UK and US sign landmark agreement," *BBC*, April 2, 2024; Ayanna Pressley from "Pressley Calls for Congress to Address Risks of Artificial Intelligence on Marginalized Communities," *pressley.house.gov*, March 21, 2024; Jules White from "Need to get a grip on AI? There are classes for that," *Marketplace*, March 14, 2024.

Library of Congress Cataloging-in-Publication Data is available at www.loc.gov or upon request from the publisher.

ISBN: 979-8-89232-760-2 (hardcover)
ISBN: 979-8-89232-937-8 (paperback)
ISBN: 979-8-89232-847-0 (ebook)

For more information, write to Bearport Publishing, 5357 Penn Avenue South, Minneapolis, MN 55419.

Contents

Tech Tutor

Need help with your homework? Try an online tutor. Type in your question. Within seconds, you could get a long, detailed answer. How is this possible? The tutor might not be a person. It could be a machine using artificial intelligence (AI).

Alan Turing was a mathematician in the 1940s. He believed machines could be trained to learn. This laid the groundwork for artificial intelligence.

Alan Turing

Supersmart Machines

AI is computer **software**. Advanced AI systems let machines do humanlike tasks.

AI is helping tech get closer to human intelligence. It lets computers and robots solve problems. With AI, some computers can act without being told what to do.

Machine learning allows computers to build on what they know. They look at what happened in the past. Then, they change to do better in the future. This is a lot like how humans make decisions.

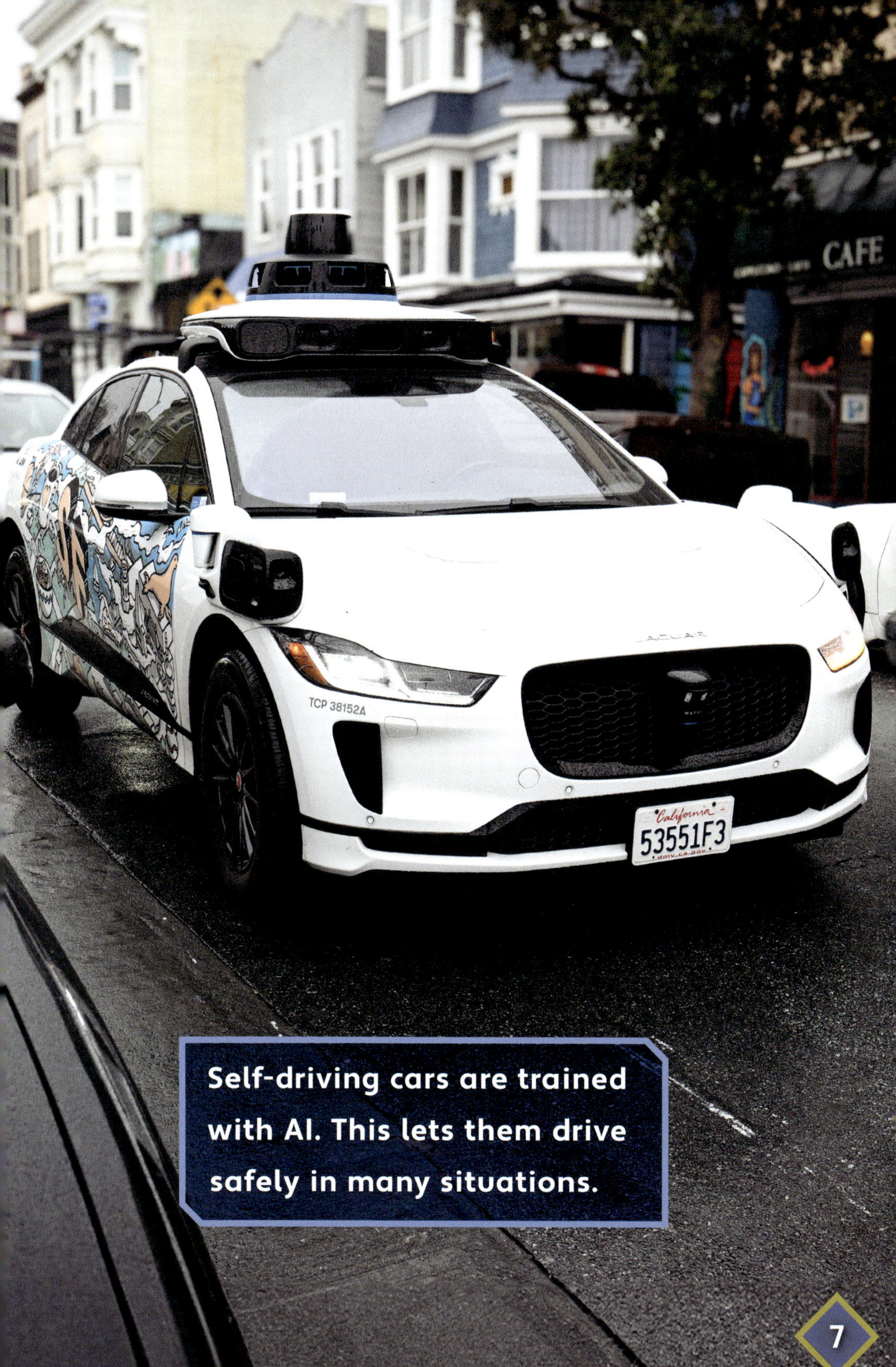

Self-driving cars are trained with AI. This lets them drive safely in many situations.

How do these machines become smart? It starts with a lot of information. People feed **data** into a computer. They may give the computer writing, coding, or images.

The AI organizes the data. It finds patterns. Over time, the computer learns what to look for.

Training AI often includes **feedback** from people. The computer is told when it gets things right. If it does something wrong, it gets that feedback, too.

Often, it takes many computers working together to train an AI system.

Learning Language

With enough training, AI helps machines do what was once impossible. Natural language processing (NLP) is a kind of AI that lets machines learn human language. It learns from written or spoken data. Large language models (LLMs) are NLP **programs** with lots and lots of data.

Computers use languages, too. This is how people who make software tell computers what to do. However, computer languages are different from human ones. Many use numbers and symbols.

Creating Content

Generative AI takes things a step further. It makes new content using what it learned.

Some generative AI uses LLMs to do even more. A human gives the AI a **prompt**. They ask the tech to do something. The computer answers in a way that looks and sounds like human language.

Some generative AI can make pictures from prompts. This AI needs LLM training to understand written prompts. It also needs lots of image data to learn how to make images.

AI IMAGE GENERATOR
Text to Image
78%
GENERATING...

AI All Around

AI can make daily life easier. It is used in autofill and autocorrect data. Smart assistants use LLMs to learn to follow directions and answer questions. Many customer service phone numbers are answered by AI-trained computers. All of this saves human power.

Have you ever thought about something only to start seeing ads for it online? AI may be behind that. Some companies are using AI-powered technology to learn what you are interested in.

Siri, Alexa, and Bixby are all smart assistants.

At a doctor's office, AI can save lives. It can go through lots of health data quickly. If someone is sick, AI can look for similar cases. It can help doctors figure out what is wrong. This is often faster than if a doctor were to work alone.

AI may also help stop the spread of illnesses. Some AI programs can track where a sick person has been. Then, they warn others who shared the same spaces.

A Smart Choice?

With all it can do, artificial intelligence can seem smart. However, it's not actually intelligent. Generative AI makes things based on patterns. It guesses what will come next. That means it does not really know an answer. Sometimes, it gives text or data that sounds true but isn't.

The false things AI makes up are called **hallucinations**. If these responses aren't fact-checked, people may believe they are true. They may act on this bad information.

Some people are worried about the **ethics** of AI. The data that trains AI is pulled from many people's work. Some companies have used **copyrighted** materials for training. Yet, the people who made the original content are not paid or credited. Is this fair?

Generative AI can make art in the same style as a famous painter. It can also write stories that sound like they are by well-known authors.

This image made using AI is based on art by Vincent van Gogh.

Bad Data, Bad AI

AI needs data for training. However, data coming from people can be **biased**. It may favor some groups. It could create problems for others. That data teaches AI to act in the same way. Then, the technology further spreads the bias.

Some medical data is about only certain groups of people. For example, many early drug studies included only men. Medical advice based on this data may not work for women.

If data does not include differences, AI may think everyone is the same.

Can't Keep Up

AI is changing very quickly. It is getting faster and more humanlike. This makes some people worried.

Many want to limit what can be used to train AI. Others think about how AI should or should not be used. Laws about artificial intelligence are having a hard time keeping up.

Personal information is sometimes used in AI training. But this data isn't always kept safe. Laws may be needed to protect people from data leaks.

Lawmakers need to learn about AI before they make rules about it.

The Future of AI

AI is advancing. As it does, people are looking for new ways to use it. Some researchers are training humanlike robots. AI helps the robots do things humans can do. Soon, even more will be possible.

Some AI researchers are working to join tech and people. They are trying to combine human brain cells with computer systems. Someday, there could be brains that are part human, part robot.

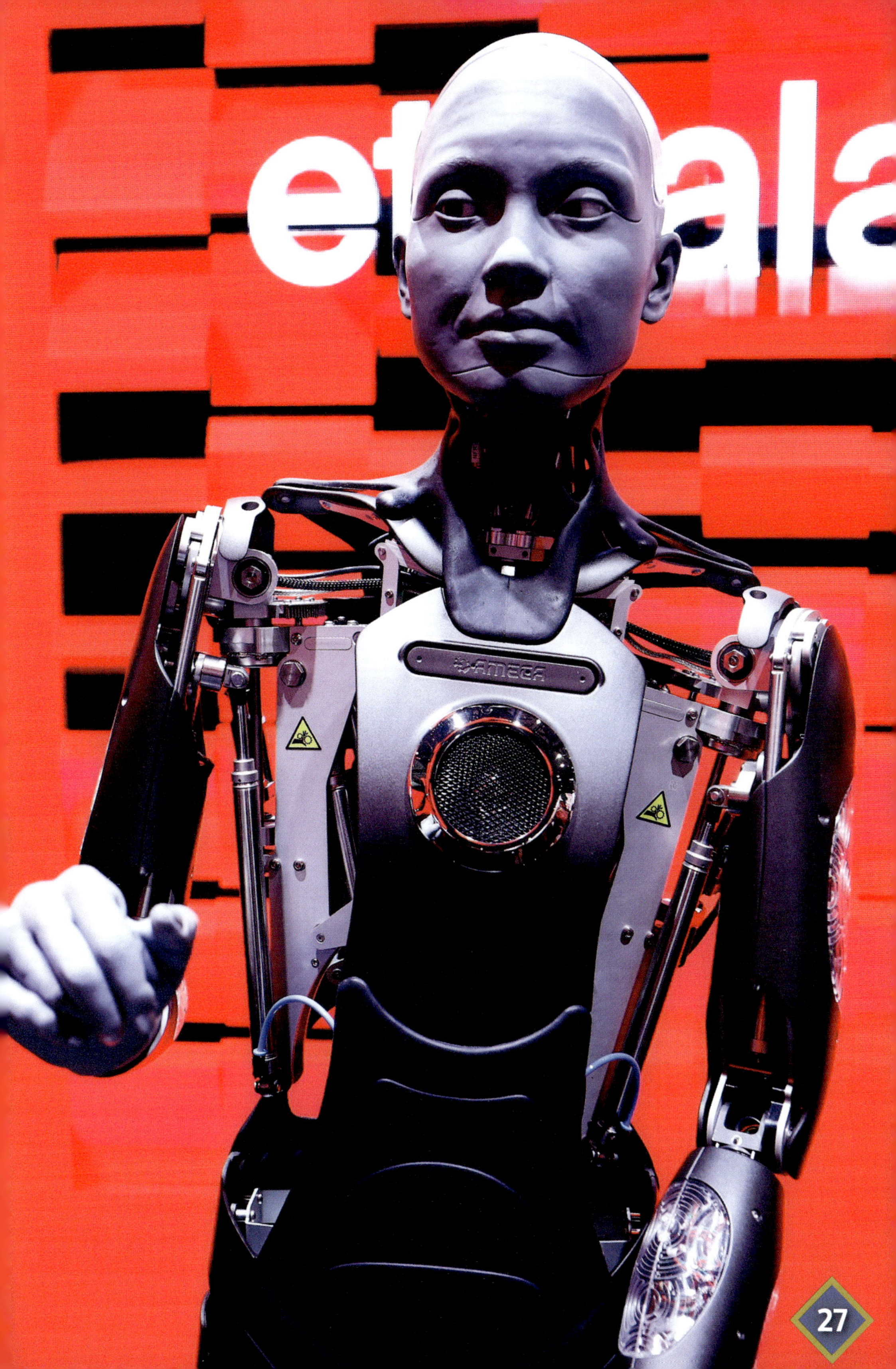
AMECA

Voices in the News

People have many things to say about AI. Some of their voices can be heard in the news.

Nigel Shadbolt
Computer science professor, University of Oxford

“AI . . . can be weaponized and used for good or ill.”

Ayanna Pressley
U.S. House Representative

“While AI presents opportunities for progress, it also poses significant risks.”

Jules White
Computer science professor, Vanderbilt University

“This is a . . . moment in computing, where anybody can . . . have the power of a programmer without having to know how to program.”

SilverTips for SUCCESS

★ SilverTips for REVIEW

Review what you've learned. Use the text to help you.

Define key terms

bias
data
generative AI
large language models
machine learning

Check for understanding

What is AI?

How do people train AI?

Why might AI make mistakes?

Think deeper

How do you use AI in your life? What are some of the benefits and drawbacks of using it?

★ SilverTips on TEST-TAKING

- **Make a study plan.** Ask your teacher what the test is going to cover. Then, set aside time to study a little bit every day.
- **Read all the questions carefully.** Be sure you know what is being asked.
- **Skip any questions** you don't know how to answer right away. Mark them and come back later if you have time.

Glossary

biased favoring one person or point of view over another

copyrighted protected under the law as being owned by someone

data information

ethics sets of moral values

feedback a reaction to something that has been done

generative made based on a prompt in response to a broad set of data

hallucinations false or misleading responses made up by an AI system

programs groups of instructions that can do many things on a computer

prompt a set of instructions or something that causes action

software something on a computer with a set task

Read More

Drimmer, Stephanie Warren. *Ultimate Book of the Future: Incredible, Ingenious, and Totally Real Tech That Will Change Life As You Know It.* Washington, D.C.: National Geographic, 2022.

Finan, Catherine C. *Technology (X-treme Facts: Science).* Minneapolis: Bearport Publishing, 2021.

Simons, Lisa M. Bolt. *Super Surprising Trivia about Artificial Intelligence (Super Surprising Trivia You Can't Resist).* North Mankato, MN: Capstone Press, 2024.

Learn More Online

1. Go to **FactSurfer.com** or scan the QR code below.
2. Enter "**Artificial Intelligence**" into the search box.
3. Click on the cover of this book to see a list of websites.

Index

About the Author

Ashley Kuehl is an editor and writer specializing in nonfiction for young people. She lives in Minneapolis, MN.